Fall in Love
with
BLOGGING
FROM PASSION TO PLAN TO PROFIT

by Dwainia Grey

Published by
GreyChild Communications
Toronto, ON

Fall in Love with Blogging / Dwainia Grey
ISBN-13: 978-0995165014
ISBN-10: 0995165017

This book is dedicated to my my son that drives me through the chaos.

Table of Contents

INTRODUCTION

Introduction

Did you know that websites with blogs get 55% more visitors and generate 67-88% more leads?

For many a blog seems to be one more tool to add to the to-do list. A dreaded task.

A blog is more than a marketing tool it's a way to express yourself, showcase your expertise, and start a movement with your purpose.

This book and workbook are for conscious entrepreneurs to build your blog around your passion, create and implement a plan and monetize your blog to start seeing profits.

A blog based on your passion is a great way to build your Awesome Nation and fulfill your life's purpose.

Your blog is central to your online marketing and can be central to your sales funnel. It's a way to get more eyes on your offers, more leads in your pipe and more dollars in your bank account.

An Empowerpreneur blog is a way to reach your readers and clients, and offer free, valuable information. It's another avenue to empower others. It's a way to connect and build relationships. And it's a way to make money.

This book and companion workbook is a guideline, a base for you to develop your own strategies based on what works best for your readers and you. It's a step-by-step from passion, to plan to profit.

Why Blog?

What if your blog post can change someone's life for the better?

With a passion centered blog you can provide information to someone at the exact moment they need it. Whether its's 2am in the morning, your blog can provide much-needed information. Not only will someone find answers, but they will also find you.

Picture this: someone has a challenge or problem that they use search engines to find the answer to. Your expert blog post shows up in the results. Your blog post title and description is an exact match to what they are looking for because you search engine optimized the post.

Because you did your research on your preferred client, you understand their pain, and you post offers results / solutions. You are now an authority in their eyes.

They check out the rest of your branded blog that has awesome design and more valuable content. They immediately signup for your awesome opt-in and/or share your blog post on social media.

They continue to visit your blog and read your emails, where you share product / service information, how-to's and answer reader / client questions. They now begin to know, like and trust you. They are ready to buy from you or hire you.

Your blog can be a 24/7 marketing tool and shop where you can share valuable content and turn readers into buyers.

SECTION ONE

Passion

What's Your Passion?

Passion gets you out of bed in the morning.
Passion pushes you to try new things.
Passion empowers you.
Passion can fuel you.
Passion will bring you to the top.

What do you feel passionate about?

What do you love?

What can you talk non-stop about?

If money was not a factor what activity can you do all day, every day?

• What are your hopes, and dreams and wishes?
• What are you good at?
• What are your strengths?

Review your past and current hobbies, work, family life, and relationships. What excites you the most?

What is the problem that you're most passionate about solving or helping with through the work you do? How can you centre your blog around this?

What's the issue that drives you crazy that you want your blog to be a solution for?

The most successful and fulfilling blogs are about what people are passionate about. The next level of blogging success is lifestyle. How can you blog about your passion? Live your passion?

A passion centered blog inspires and motivates you. A passion centered blog is sustainable. A passion centered blog guides you. Every decision, every choice you make from planning to profit is guided by your passion.

What passion is your blog about?

Your Why

People don't buy what you do, they buy why you do it. - Simon Sinek

What's your why? You have defined your passion that your blog is about, now turn your focus to your why.

What is the deeper meaning behind what you do?

I want to help _____ (your blog audience) get _____ (specific result) because it will help their life in what way _____ and this is important to me because _____ (how you want the world to change).

Why do you want to share this passion with others?

How will your blog change lives? What are the issues, challenges, mistakes, life lessons that drive you to do what you do? What is your purpose?

Building a solid blog has a lot to do with the mission and vision of your business. Your vision and mission are both a part of the blogging for business process. What is your vision for your business? How does your blog tie in? All business / blogging decisions must remain true to your vision and mission.

Values
Before you define your mission and vision, decide on your blog values.

Vision
What is your vision? A concrete vision makes you think about the bigger picture and what you really want, and it should help "pull" you forward.

Your vision is fluid, whatever vision you write down today WILL change... and that's OK.

What is your Vision in 5 Years?

Mission
Your mission (or purpose) statement is what gives your blog heart.
How will you accomplish your vision?

Your Gift

The meaning of life is to find your gift.
The purpose of life is to give it away.
- Pablo Picasso

Is your business designed around your passion?
Combine your passion and your gifts and start making money.

The Sweet Spot is the intersection of what you're passionate about + your natural strengths + the problem that you can solve for your preferred client (what you can get paid to do).

Whatever you offer, free, paid, big ticket should come from your sweet spot.
1. Lead Generating Offer (Free Gift)
2. Discovery Session
3. Programs (Results-oriented systems)
4. Products (Do It Yourself Systems)

Your Gifts / Your Strengths
- What are you good at?
- What do you do that excites you?
- In your past and current work experience:
    - What did you love doing?
    - What skills did you acquire?
    - What are you known for?

If you are still stuck read *Now Discover Your Strengths* by Marcus Buckingham. Online there is a huge amount of noise and competition. With many similar blogs out there you may think, why join the party? Don't worry about who is already out there. Your gifts are unique to you. You are the only one that will do it the way you do. You are the only one that will blog in your unique voice. Your passion centred blog will attract the right people that want to connect with you, share your expertise and life experiences in the voice that only you can share.

Doing What Matters

When do you feel powerful, passionate, free, incredibly useful, inspired? Danielle Laporte

Why do you care?

To be a successful Empowerpreneur blogger, you need to define what your blog is about. Why do you care about your blog, your audience, and your topic? It's important to ensure you blog about what matters to you.

A passion centered blog, backed by your powerful why and enhanced with your gifts is a recipe for finding your bliss and success.

Do what you love, and you'll never work another day in your life.

Fall in love with blogging means loving what you do. If you are blogging your passion, blogging your why, sharing your gifts, blogging is easy, and it becomes your obsession.
Action: Write down your passion you can easily blog about.

SECTION TWO

Plan

Objective

What Are Your Blogging Goals and Objectives?

Your passion centered blog is part of a bigger picture. If you picked up this book, you are blogging for business, and the end game is to make profits as well as help people. What are your business objectives? How will a blog help you achieve these objectives?

A blog provides a great focal point for your social media, content marketing, and search optimization. To maximize the impact of your blog, focus on your mission and vision.

Your blog must reflect you and your business and provide value. What information do you want to share with as many people as possible? What problem or challenge can your blog help solve?

To create and sustain a successful blog you need to clarify your blogging goals.

What are your top three goals for your blog?
Determine your goals for blogging. What do you want to accomplish as a result of your investment in your blog?

- Build a platform
- Become a celebrity
- Increase your reach
- Build your brand
- Increase customer loyalty
- Establish credibility

- Improve customer service
- Generate leads and sales
- Convert leads to sales

As an Empowerpreneur, you must set goals for yourself and your business and then make the two align.
What do you want to accomplish personally in the next 90 days that relate to your blog / business?

How does your blog fit into your life's goals?

Setting Goals

You have defined your blog topic (your passion), your why and what gifts you plan to sell now it's time to set goals.

- A blog builds trust, generates interest, gains credibility and loyalty.
- A blog is a source of leads, and sales.
- A blog can make you famous.

How do you know if your blog is a success?

Set income goals (See Plus & Minuses), blog engagement goals (See Blogging for Engagement), blog traffic goals (See Blog Traffic) and list building goals.

Make it measurable.
What is the ultimate goal you can achieve to know you have made it? Write down your top 3 big reach for the sky goals for your blog.

Next, create your one year goal that moves you towards your top 3, now break it down into quarterly goals. Break down your quarterly goals into monthly goals.

Monthly Goals

Your monthly goals should be a combination of KPI - Key Performance Indicators (read section on metrics) and the monthly goal that leads to your pie in the sky goals.

Preparing to Blog

Blogging for business is not a get rich quick solution. You have to be in it for the long haul. Acknowledge and celebrate the minor and major successes.

You also have to roll with setbacks and be prepared for disappointments. Most entrepreneurs have dealt with anxiety, overwhelm, and uncertainty but a blogger also has to contend with writer's block and self-doubt.

As an Empowerpreneur, you also have to deal with maintaining your energy levels.

Being prepared to handle the issues of an entrepreneur, empowerpreneur and blogger can be exhausting.

- Join a support group and / or mastermind
- Join groups on social media
- Be active away from your computer.
- Get out of the house / office.
- Set boundaries.
- Stay positive.
- Develop a self-care weekly routine.

- Scheduling, automation and batching are your friends.
- Prioritize.
- Get help. build your team and outsource
- Set, track, and monitor objectives, goals and metrics.
- Schedule vacation, and me-time.
- Plan for business and self-development.

Plan. Plan. Plan.

Plan for success.
Plan your blog posts (Review 52 Weeks)
Plan your blog writing and publishing schedule.
Plan products, services and launches.
Plan for multiple streams of income.
Plan your finances - budget, savings, taxes, emergency fund, income, and expenses.

Action: Write down your blog goals and objectives.

Blog Planning

Blog Topic

In Section 1, we reviewed your passion, your why and your gifts. Now you want to build a blog that is passion centred that can help you connect with others while leading them to buy your gifts. Why do you want (or have) a blog? What kind of information or knowledge do you want to share? Who is the preferred reader for your blog?

Based on your passion what type of blog do you want to have:

Niche - Blogs that have very narrow focus and very specific. Earn expert status with laser targeted posts and targeted audience.

Lifestyle / Personal - A lifestyle blog focused on your interests such as fashion, food, beauty, travel music, etc. Or a personal blog about your life story, or a journal.

Strictly Business
Main objective is to support your business or sales.

Cause / Non-Profit
Support your cause or promote a non-profit.

Platform Builder
Normally for an author or speaker to build name recognition and personal brand.

Blog Host
Welcome guest bloggers. You become the editor / curator.

Combination
Can be any combination of the above.

Before you decide on a blog type and topic ensure that this is where your heart lies because you want to be able to continuously write valuable content and don't want to eventually lose interest in your blog. Choosing a blog type and topic does not mean you shouldn't blog about general and unrelated topics that have broad appeal that can even take your blog to next level it just helps with focus and blog planning.

Also when choosing a blog type and topic think of your preferred client / reader (more in the next section). Why should they read your blog? What is the benefit of your blog? How will it help them? What problem are you helping them solve? And what is your solution?

Brainstorm blog topics that are passion centred, around selling your gifts and providing solutions to your preferred client.

Once you choose a main blog topic, create 5-7 sub-topics as categories for your blog.

How You Relate To Your Audience

Don't focus on having a great blog. Focus on producing a blog that's great for your readers. – Brian Clark

Your Preferred Client™

As part of your blog planning, you must know who you want to reach and why.

Define your preferred client. It's easy to write your blog posts when you focus on one person.

Your Preferred Client is NOT the only person you will work with.

Your preferred client IS the only kind of person you will spend your marketing time, marketing energy, and marketing dollars attracting to your business.

If you market for everyone, you market to no one.

Who is Your Preferred Client?
• The people you most want to work with.
• The people that resonate with your passion.
• The people who want, need and are willing to pay for what your business provides.
• Can you find them?

The Success Factor™
• How do they define success and failure?
• What's keeping them from their goals?
• What are perceived obstacles to their success?
• What are actual obstacles to their success?

• Use your blog to provide information to help your preferred client succeed.

Knowing and understanding your client allows you to provide better solutions as well as craft your blog posts to the issues.

Use Problem and Solution on Your Blog

Problems - Write a description of the problem your preferred client is experiencing, as it relates to your business / blog / passion. This isn't what **you** think the problem is, it's what **they** think it is! Remember, "It's Not About You, It's About Them"

• What is the primary problem they have, as it relates to your business?
• What are the consequences to them in not solving this problem?
• What keeps them from solving this problem on their own?
• What outcomes/return on investment do they expect from your services or products?

BONUS - each of the points of above can be addressed in multiple blog posts.

You need to learn what words or phrases the clients use to describe the problem and find solutions to the problem. Using these keywords in your blogging to help you be found.

Symptoms - What are the symptoms they experience? Think of what they are seeing, thinking, feeling or hearing... Again, this is as if you are walking in their shoes, not your own.

Results / Solution - Having a successful blog means providing value. Not only do you want to guide people to buy the products and services you promote on your blog you want to offer solutions on your blog as well.
What problems can you solve and how can you alleviate the symptoms they have?
How can you use your blog to help solve their challenges and achieve their goals?
What skills, tools and knowledge can you help them with? Use your blog as a resource centre for your readers.

How can you use your blog to let people know what they can expect to experience by working with you?

Use you blog to address and identify the most common objections/concerns your Preferred Client might have about investing in your services or products.

The Buying Process
Learn about your preferred clients buying process. Do they research potential purchases online? (If so, where?) Do they make the buy decision alone? Your preferred reader may also be on different levels of the buying process depending on need. Your reader may need it now (use urgency), may know they need it but not ready to buy, may be browsing and want information. By writing to every level of the buying process, you increase your chances of generating leads and sales. Knowing where your client is in the buying process and how they decide to purchase is a plus when drafting your blog posts and website sales copy.

Your Preferred Client Avatar

To have a solid understanding of who your target audience is and understand what their needs, interests, and goals delve into the demographics of your preferred reader / client. Use the information above including the demographics to create your Preferred Client Avatar. Give your Avatar a name and create all your blogging content directed to your Preferred Client Avatar.

Meet Linda, my Preferred Client Avatar. Linda is a 38-year-old petite blonde. She is married and a mother of two beautiful girls. Linda is a reiki master, nutritionist, and speaker on wellness. She is the buyer and manages the finances in the family. Linda wants to do less one-on-one consulting and move to online courses. To do this Linda wants a new website and a blogging strategy. She is worried that by making this transition, her family will have less money. Linda is a perfect candidate for my Awesome Nation Allure program and the Awesome Nation Engagement Program. Linda can also become a consulting client. If Linda does not want to do it on her own she can choose my DFY – Done for You Services where we create her website and manage her blogging.

Action:
Create your preferred client avatar.

Research

Research is important for bloggers.

1. Research your target audience
2. Research your niche influencers
3. Research for blog posts.

Research your target audience. In addition to the demographic and psychographic information you have already collected, it's beneficial to do your market research.

The Internet makes it super easy to find data on just about any niche or segment of the population you can think of.
In addition to the web you can use:
- Surveys/Questionnaires/Polls
- Interviews
- Observation
- Focus Groups
- Industry/Association Reports
- Your Competitors
- Complete Market Research Worksheet
- Current Client Perception

You can't please everyone. Your goals, marketing, and energy all align to reach your preferred client. Understanding your preferred client brings clarity to your business and makes it easy to write content and marketing materials.

The other side of your research and to find out where your target audience is to market to them; look at influencers in your niche.

Industry Influencers
Start following your preferred clients interests and influencers as well as blogs your preferred client reads.
Do a regular search for keywords and questions that they use to find you.

Watch other businesses related to your business, and that are complementary to your business.

When looking for influencers to share their content you want real people that blog and real people that engage on social media.

Review how often they post, what they post about and what hashtags they use

1. Use them as a source of inspiration as well as a source for blog posts. Create blog posts that refer to influencers.

2. Engage with influencers (Share their content, like and comment on social media and their blogs). People who share great content, get as much credit as the originator and you become a source that people go to for information.

3. Comment on their blog posts

Building strong relationships with influencers and other bloggers is key to getting your blog noticed and found.

Make connecting with other bloggers a priority. You will find opportunities to collaborate and guest post. Reach out to bloggers that cater to the same audience as you do base on interests, niche, and industry.
Every week make time to read about not only your industry but also the interests of your preferred client.

If you are not keeping up to date, you are doing a disservice to your clients. You should be on top of the latest news and trends in your industry.

Take time each week, daily is best for research. Using tools like Feedly and bloglovin to gather blogs of interests is a huge time saver.

Blog Post Research
Not all blog posts need help with research. It's useful for longer blog posts.

Some of you bloggers require facts to back up your claims. It's good to allow time for research. Also, have "go to sources" on hand to be a source for your blogs.

Consistency & Frequency

In the last chapter, you established your goals for your blog. Keep those goals in mind, especially when you're getting started. It can be tough to get traffic and comments happening on your blog, but don't give up! Remember how your blog fits into the bigger picture of your business.

And keep these two rules in mind:
1. Your blog is a work in progress. You can adapt as you go.

2. Never think of your blog as finished. Instead, think of it as a growing, developing part of your online marketing that can be modified and tweaked as you go.

Be flexible about your schedule, your types of posts, and adjust as you need to. This book is a guideline, a base for you to develop your own strategies. As you go along you will learn what your target audience responds to best and what works for you.

Be consistent: Don't post sporadically and expect to maintain the momentum you built. Keep top of mind by creating a schedule and being consistent.

Be frequent: Posting frequently on your blog attracts repeat visitors, and builds trust. The more frequently and consistently you blog – Google will love you! Google loves new content.

Be present: Respond promptly to comments on your blog and email messages. As part of your service policy incorporate a response time. No matter what consider all interaction good or bad as an opportunity.

Action: Write down your blog post frequency - how often do you plan to blog?

Plus and Minuses

Blogging for Business means treating your blog as a business and that means tracking and understanding your financials.

Step 1: **Review Goals.** Create a revenue goal for the next 12 months. How will you meet this goal? Know how many sales of each offering you will need to accomplish your revenue goals.

Step 2: **Blog Budget.** Create a blog budget. Write down all projected expenses related to the blog. For example: cost of web hosting and web maintenance. Be sure to include development and marketing expenses. Also, calculate your estimated profit or loss based on projected revenues and estimated expenses.

Step 3: **Tracking**. Track your actual income and expenses.

Step 4: **Pay Yourself First.** Even if you start out paying only $25 a week. Get in the habit of paying yourself.

Step 5: **Taxes.** Prepare for taxes. Know what your tax obligations are and set aside money to cover your taxes.

Every month set a realistic revenue goal. What 3 activities can you do in that month to achieve that goal? How many reviews do you need to write? Do you need to find and solicit new sponsors? What affiliate programs do you need to promote? Are you launching a new product or program?

Treat your blog like a business and plan for expenses by creating a comprehensive budget. Knowing your numbers are important, so you need to track all income and expenses. It kills me when I ask business owners how much are they making from their blog and they don't know.

WordPress

There are many content management platforms out there that are built for blogging, but I recommend WordPress especially if you are just starting out. Why? Because it's easy. Creating a blog post is as easy as using a word processing program.

Not only is WordPress one of the easiest platforms to use, but search engines also love it because it's search engine friendly. Here are the top 5 reasons to use WordPress.

1. WordPress is Free. I recommend you use the self-hosted option to own your own domain and content. With the self-hosted option, you only have to pay for your domain and hosting because the WordPress CMS is free to use.

2. WordPress is Customizable. With the use of plugins and themes and a great web designer / developer you make WordPress look, however, you want and do whatever you want.

3. WordPress is scalable. You can run a small blog, an e-commerce site or a content publishing empire. The New York Times, CNN, Forbes, Mashable, and many others use WordPress for their sites.

4. WordPress is a Content Management System by definition. It comes with its own built-in scheduler, so you can even schedule blog posts for two or more years if you wanted to. WordPress makes it easy to post, update and edit posts on any computer using any browser. It also allows for multiple users, authors, and editors.

5. WordPress is Media Friendly. You are able to add video, audio, and images with ease. Also allows for embeds from popular sites such as YouTube.

Once you have the foundation of your blog ready, it's time to set up and configure your Wordpress website. (Or reconfigure if you already have a blog)

1. Set-up the blog
2. Add and configure your plugins
3. Get a custom theme to match your branding
4. Configure for SEO
5. Start blogging

There are many great guides to get you started blogging. You can grab a quick guide or follow the blog posts at TorontoWPExpert.

Mobile

Fact: Mobile device ownership is set to outpace desktop computers. Use your analytics to verify the increase of both smartphones and tablets accessing your blog. Many people all over the world have smartphones and access to Internet.

Mobile marketing gives you access to both local and global markets on a major scale.

Ensure that your blog is mobile friendly. You can create a mobile version of your blog or better yet ensure that your site has a responsive design - optimal viewing on the website, tablet or phone.

It's important to understand how users interact with your content on a mobile device and how to optimize that experience.

Must Have Web Pages

In addition to writing an Awesome blog, there are some pages that every blogger needs to have. Your blog posts provide valuable information while these must have pages serve as explainer pages and delve into details about who you are and your why. These pages help you build credibility, provide better user experience and increase conversion.

About Page - After the home page, the second most visited page is your About Me page. People buy from people. The About page is a great page to start building trust. People want to know more about the blog author. This page also helps with branding and makes your blog more personal.

Craft an awesome bio that allows people to get to know you and understand your why. Share your enthusiasm for you passion through the About page. (Read Section "Craft a Better About Me Page")

Home Page - The home page must be able to convey who you are, your why and what your selling in 3 seconds since the attention span on the web is 3 seconds.

Use your home page to quickly convey:
• Who is your preferred client
• What they are struggling with
• What they want instead
• What's possible
• How you help them

Ensure your home page has a call to action. The number of websites that are beautifully designed with no clear call to action is a crime. Be clear about the objective of your website and tell visitors what you want them to do.

Optimize Your Home Page by using blog excerpts instead of full blog posts, use pagination and minimize the use of large images and video. Ensure your home page is not only attractive to keep people on your website but easy to navigate.

The less content you have on the home page – the faster it loads.

Start Here - Not every blogger includes this page, but it is a great page to include that leads the blog visitors where you want them to go. You can start the page with a brief description of your blog and then list categories with articles under them to make it easy for people to find what they are looking for. It serves as a table of contents or index to your blog. With a Start Here page, people spend more time on your blog, and you have a lower bounce rate. End the page with an opt-in box. This page may be your biggest conversion page from reader to subscriber.

The biggest bonus of this page is that you can ensure that you reach people at any level of the buying cycle. You can include blog posts for people who are ready to buy now and blog posts for the people that are just beginning their research.

This page is great for increasing traffic and improving SEO.

Resource Page - This is another page that not every blogger includes but if you want to monetize your blog this is a great page to start with. You can include a list of free and paid resources to help visitors to your site. You want to make this page has everything for beginners to expert level visitors. Include a short description of the products and services you use along with affiliate links and links to your products and services. Also If you have written review posts, you should include these links.

Work With Me - If you are providing services, in addition to sales pages (more later), you need to include a Work With Me page. This page serves as a summary of your services and a big call to action to work with you.

Describe the services / packages you offer with emphasis on benefits and results, have a clear call to action and add testimonials. Keep in mind your preferred client avatar when building this page and make it personable.

Testimonial Page - A big credibility booster to selling your own products and services is a dedicated testimonial page. Testimonials should be from actual people that are willing to endorse you. Testimonials should be results-focused and include full names and headshots.

Contact Page - Nothing is worse than going to a website and having to search for contact information. Again people buy from people. It's hard to make a buying decision if you aren't able to contact the seller.
At the very least include a contact form that visitors can use to reach you.

Optional Pages
• Events - Event Calendar
• Store - Shopping Cart
• Speaking - Speakers Page
• Media - where your work has been featured, which brands you have worked with, and my current blog stats.
• Programs and services

Legal Requirements - Disclosure Policy, Privacy Policy, and Copyright

If you make money from your site, you need to have a disclosure policy. Not only is it the law, but it's also the right thing to do! A disclosure policy lets readers know you are upfront about how you are making money.

Include links to your disclosure policy page at the bottom of your sidebar and in any sponsored post or post that contains affiliate links so that people can clearly see what your policies are.

If you collect any information from readers, you must also have a privacy policy. Most advertisers require a privacy policy and may drop you if they find you don't have one. It also lets visitors know how you plan to use their information.

Don't forget the Copyright
Include copyright at the bottom of you blog. In addition, include a copyright statement that clearly lays out what's okay and what isn't when it comes to others sharing pictures and copy from your blog.

Writers Block

Plan for Writers Block. No matter how passionate you are about the topic, there may be a day when you just draw a blank. Don't panic.

Temporary solutions

- Remove distractions
- Read something unrelated (blog, magazine, or book)
- Do a physical activity
- Have a conversation
- Take a break

Get Inspired, Get Enlightened

- Brainstorming (don't analyze or create just list blog titles and topics)
- Mind Mapping (helps you generate and organize ideas)
- Your Analytics
- Your Site Search
- Check Your Alerts
- Google Keyword Planner
- Review your previous content (think series)
- Repurpose Content
- Books you read
- Ezines you subscribe to
- Blog comments
- Social Media
- Turn FAQ (Frequently Asked Questions) into blog post

Think of questions as blog titles: What, When, Where, Why, How, Why
What questions do clients ask you regularly? Use blog posts to answer them

Write about events you have attended, include pictures.
Write about challenges you've had in your business and how you overcame them.
Share your testimonials.

It doesn't hurt to take a break from blogging if you are really stuck.
Writing in batches is very important as it helps you have a library of content ready to go.
When writing, think blog series, evergreen content (never dated or loses relevancy). I have broken up a 3,000 word

evergreen post into smaller posts to have content ready for a month while on vacation.

Be prepared for times when you are unable to write or experience writer's block.

Are You Ready To Plan Your Blog?

Get Ready, Set, Go! Write your blog plan.

Are you able to commit to writing, promoting, updating and maintaining your blog?

Blogging is not just writing a bunch of posts. According to Derek Halpern of Social Triggers, 80% of being a blogger is promoting.

The reason why I created the Fall in Love with Blogging Book and Workbook is to get people to understand the work that happens behind a successful blog and to actually do the work to run a successful blog. With proper planning and strategies in place, you can focus the rest of your time on promotion.

In the next sections, we will talk about writing and scheduling. But in this section let's focus on how to get it done. The day-to-day of blog management.

How far ahead to you want to plan content?

Create an Editorial Calendar. Plan your posts several weeks in advance to avoid last minute scramble for ideas.

Set a routine for your writing.
This helps keep you on track, and you will hesitate to procrastinate. Write and schedule posts ahead of time. Create a blog writing schedule and a blog publishing scheduling.
What type of content are you going to share?
Take advantage of the different types of posts and media to make your blog more interesting.

Who will create content images, video, and copy?
Choose your blogger or if you have more than one blogger choose your editor. Someone that takes responsibility for the blog, able to manage and respond to comments and is the single point of contact.

Also keep a library of blog post ideas and sources. It's easier to start a post if you've got an idea or outline of what you're going to write.

Who will post content?
Decide how often you will publish (at least once a week). Several times a day, once a day, several times a week, once a week or else? Make a schedule and stick to it.

Who will manage marketing campaigns?
Develop a content marketing plan. How will you promote your posts/blog not only on social media? Also, develop Search Engine Optimize strategy.

Who will track, monitor and report?
On a weekly and or monthly basis review your online metrics. Learn more about your return on investment (ROI - time and money) as well as which blog posts bring in the most traffic, engagement and conversion.

Social Media

How will you use social media to promote your blog? Create a social media policy, so you can eventually delegate.

What resources will you need?

Can you do these things in-house or will you need to hire?

- Experienced Writer
- Professional Photos
- Professional Videos
- Branded Graphics

Budget - Create your blogging budget.

Startup and launch budget

Campaign budgets

Ongoing management budget

- Advertising
- Design
- Tools (Canva, Pic Monkey, Hootsuite, Buffer, etc.) Blog

Business Plan

How do you turn your passion-centric blog into a business? Start with a business plan.

By the time you complete this book, you will have a finished Blog Business Plan ready for implementation.

1. Blog Name

2. Blog Tagline

3. Blog Topic

4. Blog Purpose
What is the blog about?
A (topic) blog for (audience) to (result).

5. Blog Categories (More on Blog Categories in SEO)
5-7 categories/ subtopics that you need to talk around your topic.
Do the categories make sense to your audience?
Are the categories easy to navigate?
Are the categories displayed prominently?

6. Post Frequency
How often will you post (at least once a week)?

7. Objective
Measurable objectives in the next 6-12 months.

8. Top 3 Projects / Goals
Blog projects for the next 12 moths. Launch, ebook, redesign, etc.

9. Monthly Profit Goal
How much money do you plan to make a month from your blog?

10. Values
List your blog values.

11. Vision
Your why and plan for the future.

12. Mission
How will you accomplish your vision?

13. Your Blog in 5 Words
5 Words to describe your blog.

14. Audience
Who is your preferred reader / client?

15. Competition
List your 3 biggest competitors.

16. USP
What is your blog Unique Selling Proposition?

17. Reader Acquisition and Retention (Marketing)
How will you attract new readers and persuade them to stay and come back to your blog?

18. Your Offer
What services, products you plan to sell and what opt-ins you will offer.

19. Price Range
What is the price range of your offerings?

20. Payment Method
How do you accept payment on your blog?

Every quarter review your blog business plan. Are you in line with your objective? Have you made any changes? Do you need to make changes in order to move your blog forward? Do you need to retire or restructure any products, services, and opt-ins or content that don't match your current plan?

Download and Fill out the Blog Business Plan included in Workbook.

Blogging for Branding

Your Story

A big part of successful Empowerpreneur blogging is knowing who you are and letting others find out.

Know Your Why

What is the deeper meaning behind what you do?

I want to help _____ (your preferred client) get _____ (specific result) because it will help their life in what way _____ and this is important to me because _____ (how you want the world to change).

Use you blog to get others behind your why.

Use your blog to show why you are passionate about what you do.

Your Bio

Why do you do what you do?

How is your journey similar to your preferred client?

What adversity have you overcome that your preferred client can relate to?

Remember to establish credibility - What are some top results your clients have achieved?

Your Business

Give an overview of your business, how you got started, and what makes you thrive today. The overview should be positive and encouraging. It should also make potential clients think you are an excellent person to buy from.

Tell Your Story with Visuals
Use professional pictures of yourself on your blog. Pictures of you build familiarity and trust as they see you as a real person.

Action: Write down your story and a brief bio.

Your Voice

A successful blog is just like a really good conversation. Every person has their own voice. Use your blog, your voice to stand out and start conversations.

Be yourself, let your personality, passions, and guilty pleasures into your blog. Don't be afraid to show your quirks, pet peeves, and hard limits. Be willing to empower others by sharing your triumphs, and mistakes.

You might be tempted to look and talk like every blog out there but just be you, be authentic - true to you and standout.

How will you use your blog to show your personality?

Use your voice to tell your story and your message.
Your voice is the way only you can express yourself and your unique view of the world. Your voice shows your style, passion, and beliefs.

Find your voice and stick to it.

Eliminate Competition

Why should anyone read your blog versus the millions of other blogs out there?

In the crowded online marketing space you are competing with not only other blogs, social media, news and entertainment outlets as well as brands - Why should anyone check out your space online?

Whether you admit it or not, there will be other blogs with the same topic as you. How will your blog be different?

Niching down is a way to eliminate competition. Your niche makes you stand out in the crowd. It makes you memorable. You attract people that want the solutions you offer.

Brainstorm based on your niche what topics (categories) you will cover. Also, create regular feature posts that you know your niche will look forward to. Also, think of special features that you can link to promotions and your products.

Take the time to research competition. Learn what makes them different, and why clients should choose you. Competition isn't necessary a bad thing. It proves that there is demand.

How will you make sure your content is different from competitors? Make your content stand out and provide differentiation not only with branding but exceptional content.

Examine you competitors to see where information is missing. Fill in the gaps. Use your blog to address any problems and objections in your niche as well as fear, misconceptions, and stereotypes. Create products and services to bridge the gap. Also, promote products and services that are complimentary to yours (think affiliates)

Many businesses fail because they do not consider their competition. You need to do proper research about your competitors, learn what makes you different, why the clients should choose you, and much more.

What Makes You Different?
- What differentiates you from your competition?
- What value do you bring to your prospects?
  - How does choosing you benefit your clients?
  - Why do they like you?
  - Why do they buy from you?
- How do they use blogging? Are they successful?
- How are you similar?
- Do they have the same products and services as you?
- What types of online advertising do they use, are they successful?
- What is their campaign fails?

Action: List your top 3 competitors and do your research.

Branding

Branding is very important part of blog recognition.

Not only do you want to discover your story, find your voice and eliminate the competition, but you also want to put this all together to create a cohesive brand.

Branding is all about the image of you and your business. The concept not only includes style, colors, and logos, but also the image of perceived quality.

Branding builds trust; it motivates purchasing and builds loyalty.

Get clear on your brand message and tone before you consider color, fonts, logo, and blog design. Next, develop consistency with branded content.

When developing your brand, think about your values, mission, and vision. Know your why, your business and your story. Take into account who your preferred client is and how you want them to view your business.

Create a clear, compelling and unique **Brand Statement** - who you serve, why, kind of work you do, how you are different.

What goals or promises are you making to your readers? What are your **Blog Values**?

Personal Brand
People buy from people. Ensure your personal brand is on point with a professional headshot and bio.

Business Brand
Not only is your branding about "looking pretty", but it's also about perceived quality. Use professional email - @yourdomain.com and a business phone number.

Visual Branding increases brand recognition, loyalty and purchases. Your brand conveys who you are and is a form of communicating. What will be your tone and mood? Decide on a consistent tone - playful, serious, authoritative, joyful, and the mood you are trying to set. Are the tone and mood complimentary? How will images and content fit?

Tone + Mood + Voice
The overall feel of you brand should be consistent.

My blog is / My blog is not

List words, phrases, slang, and concepts.

Create a mood board with images, colours and design elements. A private Pinterest board is a great option to collect imagery that fit your style.

Brand Words
What adjectives best describe your brand?
When people visit your website how do you want them to feel?
What do you want people to say about your brand?
Describe your brand style. Write 3-5 words that you want to be known for.

Brand Colors
Choose 2-4 colors that convey your tone, mood, and voice. These colors will appear in your logo and are consistent on your blog.

Blog Design: Text, Titles, Graphics and Images

Use the style sheet to record Hex, RGB, and CMYK.

Brand Fonts

Fonts convey emotions formal / informal, modern / traditional, warm / cool. Choose 2-4 fonts to use on your website and images. Choose two complimentary fonts for titles / headers and text. The other complimentary fonts can be used for image overlays, social media, etc. For effective use of fonts make use of font size, font weight (bold) and other styles such as italics.

Fonts should be easy to read, so you need to take into account line height in your blog design. Too close, or too far decreases readability - consider 1.2 to 1.5 of font size.

Blog Design: Headings (Serif, short big and bold), Body (Sans-serif), Quotes

Brand Patterns are a great way to promote brand recognition. Patterns are a fun branding element that create coherence and consistency.

Blog Elements

How will you bring cohesiveness to your blog using color, fonts, patterns, and images? **Use the blog style sheet included in the Workbook to outline colors and fonts.**

1. Have a recognizable **Logo**.
Create a logo use policy; have specific guidelines for how and where logo and tagline are used and how variations are used.

2. **Title** - Why should I read? What is the promise? Use H1 tags and color to stand out.

3. **Content** - Use formatted headings (H1, H2, H3), graphics/images, bulleted lists, columns, recurring and distinct brand elements in your content

Have blogging guidelines. **Utilize blog post templates for category, series and different blog post types included in the Workbook.**

Create a blog style guide:
- Define what spellings and capitalization you will use.
- Inclusion and style of media (images, video, audio) in posts.
- Inclusion and access to downloadable resources.
- Text formatting including headings and subheadings.
- How you handle quotes, comments, and links.
- What SEO and Social Media elements to include.
- Outline the number of links per post, tweetable quotes and use of social media embeds.

4. **Images** - Have main and secondary post images for each blog category. Images of you are great for static pages. Create blog image templates utilizing text overlays, logo, and watermarks, etc., Also create social media images for blog posts.

5. **Elements** - Pattern styles, dividers , etc., Social buttons, icons, and images. Do the sidebar and footer have different graphics / images, rules, and guidelines?

When readers visit your blog they are drawn to two things:
1. How does it feel?
2. How easy is it to not only navigate but to use. Make it super easy to navigate, subscribe, comment, share and buy.

Bringing all these aspects together in a cohesive way relies heavily on the theme you choose. Choose a theme for your blog. You want a theme that is mobile compatible (responsive) and one that fits with your brand and has the tech capabilities that you want for your website. A client purchased a template that didn't allow for embedding plugins such as YouTube and wanted them to upload the videos instead which is not what they wanted. Long story short is do your research whether you are picking a template or getting a custom website you need to know what you want the website to do.

Check out other blogs and themes. See what others are doing in your niche, what do you like and what don't you like? Also look outside the box and see what other niches are doing to get inspiration.

Action: Create your blog style guide. (Worksheet included in the Blogging Workbook and Planner)

Craft a Better About Me Page

One of the most important pages on your website and the second most visited page is the "About Page".

The "About Page" can make or break a sale.

Your "About Page" isn't about you so much as it is about your preferred client and their challenges and desires, and the solution you offer that can help them achieve their goals.

The "About Page" needs to grab and keep attention of your preferred client. Use the Avatar of your preferred client to show you understand their fears, goals, and desires.

Distinguish Yourself With The About Page

You need to convey who you are, what you do and who you do it for. Get readers behind your why.

Show your personality and differentiate yourself. Use this page to make a connection and entice them to work with you and not your competition.

Include a clear call to action through out the page to lead them to what you want them to do next. Check out your services, opt-in or buy.

Don't Fall into the It's All About Me Trap

If your website especially your home page has lots of "I", "Us", "We", "Me" then you have been caught. Make use of "You" and tell your readers what they will get from working with you (result). Remember always answer "What's in it for me?"

Your "About Page" should reflect your personality and tell people who you are - people buy from people. Include your bio, credentials, and your back story (if it relates to your results) and how they can get results working with you.

Action: Create an Awesome About Page

Blog Content

Content Strategy

Content is King. Before you jump into creating a blog plan, create your content strategy. Blogging is not the only game in town, your content includes articles, social media content, video, opt-in incentives, seminars, presentations, speeches, products, programs, workshops, marketing collateral, etc.

Having top notch content makes you an authority, and this is an area you need to spend time and attention on.

Big Picture & Long-term Strategies

Preparing your content plan can take a couple of days, but the benefits are well worth the time. Create an editorial calendar that you can consult often and determine how your content will work with all your marketing strategies and convey your key message.

Create a Complete Content Strategy

- Bio and About Me page
- Blog posts
- Videos
- Newsletter
- Media pitches
- Advertisements
- Product descriptions (tell the story behind your product)
- Speaking engagements
- Teleseminars/Webinars
- Books (print books and eBooks)

Use your editorial calendar to stay ahead of your schedule and develop a bank of posts that can be used when there is a gap or you don't feel like writing or on vacation.

Remember to remain flexible and leave room for adjustment to factor in new ideas and trending topics.

Editorial Calendar

Having a plan when it comes to blogging can make or break your blog. This section is about creating and planning content.

One of the biggest challenges for most businesses with blogging is consistently coming up with original content.

By creating a plan with an editorial calendar, you can have content ready in advance and know what will be published, when and how.

Create your content calendar with something simple like an online Google calendar, an Excel spreadsheet, a Word document, desk calendar or whatever you're comfortable with. Your content calendar should include your company's events, upcoming promotions / campaigns or product launches this year. Also, add holidays and consider your sales cycles. This is not set in stone, be flexible and ready to make changes.

Begin by blocking out the dates that you want to be sure you're sharing posts around a specific event or topic and then you can see what's left to fill in.

Next, review your promotions, campaigns, and launches. You may want to have posts ready to go for the whole week about your promotion.

Review your 52-week content strategy and start filling it in. **Worksheet included in Workbook.**

Next review your calendar and for each week decide:
- What type of content will you post?
- What days of the week you will post?
- Will you use an image or video for visuals?
- Indicate which social media platform that you'll use with each blog post.

By planning ahead with dates you can refer back to, you will save time and find blogging easier to manage.

Also, an editorial is a great way to keep track of posts to reuse and repurpose.

Write Regularly
Have content to post when you don't feel like writing.
Have content ready to submit to article directories, press release, social media, and guest posts.

Action:
Create an editorial calendar for your blog.

Scheduling

A large part of planning and a time saver is scheduling blog posts.

Create Blog Posts in Batches and Schedule Your Posts

Create a blog writing schedule and a blog publishing scheduling. For some, it's overwhelming to write and publish on the same day. It also makes it so much easier to batch writing and schedule posts for publishing at a later date. Setting aside a block of time weekly to knock out your content is the best way to stay consistent, inspired, and totally ahead of the game.

1. Blog Creation - create your blog posts, images, and social media collateral in one sitting based on your editorial calendar.

Set aside time to blog daily, weekly or monthly and aim for a certain amount of words per blog post or session.

The ideal time to create content is unique to you. Some people like to wake up early, others prefer office hours while some like late nights. Know when you are most creative / productive and use it to your advantage. Nurture the perfect atmosphere to create content (home, office, coffee shop, etc.). Do flowers, candles or music get you inspired? Be prepared with all the tools you need to create including your favourite content creation beverage and snack.

2. Blog Publishing - Always publish on the same days at the same time. Providing consistent, high-quality content on a regular basis gives your blog reputation a boost and will encourage readers to become loyal.

According to the collective data of KiSSmetrics and HubSpot's Dan Zarrella, the best time to post to your blog is 11AM Monday mornings. Test your audience, post your blog at different times and different days to see when your audience is most receptive.

3. Blog Promotion - once the post has been published use tools such as Buffer and Hootsuite to schedule social media sharing.

Batching social media posts allows you to focus on engagement during the week as well as saving yourself time, effort and energy that could be better spent on serving your clients.

Scheduling allows you to be strategic about the proportion of informational posts to promotional ones as well as how much and how often you are promoting.

Prescheduling promotions is a great way to run your promotions over a specific number of days without overwhelming followers.

With your editorial calendar, you can schedule as far out as you can for static stuff like holidays and annual promotions. You can pre-schedule posts for Christmas.
It's great to have posts ready to go during the week but don't forget to monitor for timely news or trends. And promote anything new such as live events or speaking engagements.

One afternoon a week start scheduling your posts, add your promotions, blog posts, and any valuable information you curate to Buffer and Hootsuite. This is a great Sunday afternoon activity.

Action: Create a schedule for batching and scheduling your blog posts.

Va Va VooM™

Your blog is your personal network television channel but if you played commercials all day you would have a lot fewer viewers.

- Use your blog to provide value with informational posts.
- Use your blog to build relationships not only by building credibility with valuable posts but also sharing your personal life with personal posts.
- Use your blogs to increase sales by promoting what you sell.

Take the time to develop a healthy ratio of your informational posts, personal posts, and promotional posts.

Most marketing gurus toot a ratio for content marketing. How many informational posts vs promotional posts. I promote 4 aspects in my **Va Va VooM™** content marketing approach that adds visual to the list because a huge part of successful online campaigns is the eye-catching image or the must watch video. According to the stats, people are more likely to engage with images and stop to watch videos.

Value – 60% - Tips, tutorials, useful and helpful posts.

Visual – 20% - Make use of images and videos - create branded images and video. Create pinnable and shareable images for your blog.

Voice – 10% - Show your personality - personal posts about you, showing your life and a behind the scenes look.

Marketing – 10% - Promotional posts to sell and promote your products and services

Action: Start monitoring your ratio and see what works best for you.

Types of Blog Posts

Depending on your type of blog you may use a variety of blog post types to get your messages across. You may just stick to one type of posts. Review the top blog post types for Empowerpreneurs and see how it fits your blog topics and audience.

Evergreen - Evergreen posts are well researched, full of useful information and are always relevant and not trendy. Aim to publish at least one "evergreen" post quarterly and have one or two in the wings in case you can't write.
A Complete Guide To
A Beginners Guide
A to Z terms for your niche or terms that you created

List Post - Can be in the form of Tips, Top 10, Best of, Checklist, Favorites, Link Posts, etc.

Opinion Post - Give your opinion on current events, issues, and trends. Give predictions start a debate. Take a stand on your blog.

Review Post - Great for promoting your own products, sponsors, and affiliates. You can also do a comparison post, how to, before and after or recommendation. When people search for review posts, they are ready to buy.

How To - and tutorials, in general, are a great way to showcase your expertise as well as promote your products, sponsors, and affiliates. People love step-by-step and "how to" is one of the top searched terms.

Case Study - Fantastic way to showcase your business and show results.

Interview - Interview experts, other bloggers, influencers, clients, authors, etc. Great way to promote others and build relationships while providing valuable information.

Giveaways - Great way to run promotions on your blog. Giveaways can be your own product, sponsors or affiliates. You can also give away gift certificates or run a group giveaway with other bloggers.

Blog Series - Blog series are great for launches as they get people excited for your new product / service and build anticipation.

You can also do a blog series on around topics of interest. You can do a series a week, so you have a month of posts scheduled to go. Blog series are a great way to keep readers coming back and engaged.

Personal Posts - Show a day in the life, talk about lessons learned, do a behind the scenes, share something that improved your life.

Critique - Showcase your expertise and review a client's product, service, problem, or work in a blog post.

Business News - Provide news about your business, niche or industry. Write about a common misconception in your industry.

Discussion - Start a discussion or solicit feedback. Get people engaged on your blog.

Product Post - Announcements, promotions, and launches. Provide a sneak peak behind product creation. Promote your own products, affiliates, and sponsors.

Podcast or Video - Mix it up with a podcast or video.

Content Upgrades - Build your list with content upgrades. Write specific posts that you can provide additional content that adds value as a giveaway: printables, checklists, tip sheet, infographic, etc.

52 Weeks of Content

Take your blog to the next level with planning. Develop a 52-week content strategy, so you will have a post for every week of the year.

• Using your blog categories brainstorm 5 or more posts for each that you can use throughout the year.
• Using your blog categories create 3 sub-categories for each with 5 or more blog posts for each sub-category.
• Brainstorm 5 or more posts for each type of blog post.
• Brainstorm 5 or more posts that highlight your offers go even further and write down 3 post ideas for each offer.
• Review old blog posts and see where you can do upgrades by offering a free resource as an opt-in, list 5-10 blog posts where

you can add upgrades. Also, review old blog posts that you can turn into a series.

• Lastly, list 5-10 personal blog posts ideas.

Batch out your 52 in one sitting or throughout the year and have it scheduled so you have a post ready for every week of the year.

With the 52 weeks of content think traffic, engagement and leads. What topics will make people visit your website? How can you get people to interact and get the most likes, shares, and comments? How can you get people to opt-in?

Action: Write down 52 ideas you can expand on later. 52 Ideas Brainstorming Sheet is included in Workbook.

Just Write

What do I post?

People always ask what they should post on their blog. The answer is what type of blog do you have and what is your blog topic. Take into consideration your blog audience / preferred client - How can you use your blog to connect with people?

12 Steps to Writing the Perfect Blog Post

1. Determine your blog post topic and title.
Use your preferred client Avatar to develop blog posts. Write directly to your preferred client and address their fears, wants and needs. Give valuable information in the way of outcomes, solutions and results. This is the perfect opportunity to provide content upgrades. Content upgrades are a great way to

boost your opt-ins by giving away downloads and printables related to the blog post. Use blog posts as a way to squash all objections - answer every question you have ever been asked.

Write in a conversational tone in the language your preferred client speaks. Stop with jargon and being an encyclopedia.

Create a title that screams "READ ME"!

2. What is your blog post category?
Choose your SEO keyword, category, tags and hashtag(s) for your post.
A large part of blog organization and SEO is choosing the right keyword, category, tags and hashtags for each blog post. Each blog post should be optimized for one category / keyword.

3. What is the objective of your post? What is the key message? What do you want people to do? - What is your call to action?
After reading your blog post what is the main takeaway? What do you want them to know? How do yo want them to feel?

When someone reads your blog posts, what do you want them to do next? Every post should have a specific action you want your readers to take it can be as simple as "leave a comment", "download my free ebook" or "buy now".

4. What are the main ideas you want to convey?

5. Research
Stuck on what to write, do some research. Ask your readers and preferred clients in a survey what they want. Become a part of online communities, message boards, comment

threads, Facebook Groups, Twitter Chats, Google Communities, etc. where your preferred client hangs out and get inspiration.

- What questions are they asking?
- What are they complaining about?
- What do they get excited about?

Set up alerts such as Google Alerts to keep up to date and get blog ideas (industry, you, your business, your products and services, and other things related to your preferred client).

If you are quoting information let people know the source - cite the source using links (great for SEO).

6. What type of post will this be?
Settle on what type of blog post it will be.

Create posts types and templates. Decide on 3 to 5 main formats such as top 10, review, etc. Then create templates, an easy to use a formula that anyone can use. **Templates included in the Workbook**.

7. What offer / product do you want to highlight?
Create content that supports new products and services as well as existing ones. Provide useful posts that keep readers coming back for more. Use your blog to inspire, educate and engage - get readers to see themselves using your products. Get readers to feel the emotion of using your products and service.

8. Links
Not only do you want to have external links (linking sources, other bloggers, and influencers) in your blog posts, having

internal links are equally as important for SEO and keeping readers on your blog longer. Link only to relevant posts that are logical and helpful. Be authentic in your linking and remember to highlight popular posts. Link to other posts you have written, outside articles, business and referral partners, and community resources

9. Branding
Create branded posts. Does the post convey your brand message? Is it in your voice? Are you speaking directly to your preferred client? Are you using visual branding?

10. Visual / Media
Determine how you want to enhance your blog post with media. Will it be an awesome photograph, graphic, illustration or an interactive video? Give credit where credit is due and include attribution. Also, don't forget to include a branded image.

11. Social Media
Write posts that people want to share on social media and make your blog easy to share (more on this later). Every blog post should have a pinnable /shareable image.

12. Tracking
Always track links using shorteners such as bitly or the prettylink plugin, as well as traffic (page views) and engagement (comments and shares). Use your analytics to plan future blog posts.

Write, edit and publish!
Before you hit the publish button ensure you have the proper formatting, using headings and bullets as well as the correct

spelling and grammar. Read it out loud and make sure it makes sense.

The number one thing that all posts should be is valuable and useful or entertaining.

Content Curation

Curate Your Popular Content

Create a "Start Here" or "Resource" page on your website that has a mix of your most popular posts, offer posts, posts for new readers and posts that are for people along the buying spectrum (the buy now and the just looking crowd).

Use these pages to direct readers where you want them to go. Sometimes your best content will get buried, let newbies to the site find it easily.

Curate Others Content

Not only should you curate your own content. Every week you should be reading about not only your industry but also the interests of your preferred client.

If you are not keeping up to date, you are doing a disservice to your clients. You should be on top of the latest news and trends in your industry.

On a regular basis refer to other bloggers, create best of posts, write an opinion for or against another blog post. You get the picture use others content to create your own.

Use curated content to turn readers into fans into clients.

Content Repurposing

Why reinvent the wheel, repurpose your blog posts across multiple platforms and delivery methods. Save time, expand your audience, build quantity as you build quality by repurposing content.

You can turn blog posts into products and other marketing materials.

You can select blog posts and turn them into an e-book, presentations, infographics, guides, workbooks or podcast or video series. You can use these pieces as opt-ins or digital products to sell as well as content upgrades.

You can also create a program (or group program) around your blog content with added bonuses and worksheets and include one-on-one, or weekly group webinars.

You can also repurpose blog posts into emails series and guest blog posts series.

You can also use old content to create buzz on social media with awesome graphics and infographics.

On a regular basis review your editorial calendar for older content for repurposing and refreshing.

Search Engines and Readers love it when you update a post. When I see a post that says it was updated recently or contains new information I will read it to see what's new.

• You can change the title for an updated Search Engine Optimized post.

- Add a content upgrade
- Change the introduction and/or conclusion
- Add more depth with examples, pictures, and facts
- Update content with current information and facts
- Update dead links
- Add a new call to action

On a regular basis review your offline marketing materials and company information. How can you turn these into blog posts? You can turn case studies, presentations, interviews, newsletter articles, etc. into blog posts.
When creating any and all content be proactive and think how you can repurpose.

Action: Create a repurpose plan for each piece of content.

Blog Format

Format your blog post for readability, shareability, and SEO.

When formatting always write to your preferred client / audience. Mix evergreen posts with trendy to get maximum impact. Aim for shareability. How can you add so much value that your readers want to share your posts on social media and with others?

When formatting and writing keep in mind the needs, issues, values, challenges of your preferred client. Solve problems think results. How can you format and present the information to quickly and easily convey "What's in it for me"?

Start with an awesome keyword rich title. Ensure your title is compelling and attracts the right people. Take the time to craft the right SEO title and description. If your blog post comes up in search results you want to make readers click and read immediately.

Longer posts are read more and indexed better. The most shared posts are evergreen posts that are usually 3,000 to 10,000 words long. These posts can drive traffic for years to come. However, don't discount the short post. A shorter post with useful information can quickly go viral. Aim for posts 500 to 1,000 words (minimum 300 words for SEO). Vary blog posts length.

Make blog posts scannable. Remember online you have 3 seconds to make an impression. People scan articles for the important points because they don't want to take time to read anymore. Utilize headers, 3-4 sentence paragraphs, and bullet points; it makes it easier to read and breaks up text. Be bold for emphasis, italics when used properly are also great for making text stand out.

For a more interactive post and to solicit emotion use images.

Always include a call to action - no call to action is a road leading nowhere.

Feature other people - quotes, opinions, guest blogging from others, media, professionals, bloggers, influencers and clients. People love to be mentioned.

Always check spelling and grammar, triple check facts, and links.

Remember repackage and repost. Rewrite, shorten it, expand it to share with other formats and others places.

I recommend you create templates for the different types of blog posts you create to make it easier to create content. The Blogging Workbook and Planner feature blog planners (templates) for different types of posts such as regular blog post, giveaway post, review post and more.

Media

The right image can invoke an emotional response solidifying connections and increasing interaction. People are more likely to watch and share video (vlogging), while audio is still not mainstream allowing you stand out (podcast).

Relevant media used properly can enhance reader experience and give search engines more context to rank your website.

Use images, video and audio on your website to encourage engagement, increase reach and show your passion and personality.

Images should be search engine optimized with keyword optimized name, alt tags and title tags. Optimize images by sizing them to fit the space on your blog before uploading. Images can also support your branding, add a watermark, logo or URL to your images. **Use the Image Planner included in the Workbook**.

It's best to host your videos on video sharing websites like Youtube to get more exposure. Video must be keyword optimized for SEO to get found online. Videos should be informative, and entertaining with the goal of going viral. Brand your video with an intro and outro.

The best podcasts are interviewed based. Interview people that can help your preferred client look at influencers, other bloggers and related interests of your preferred client. Think results, inspiration, and motivation when interviewing. Publish your podcast on websites like iTunes or SoundCloud to get more exposure.

When using media in your blog, aim to reach your preferred client, and always optimize for SEO.

Action: Ensure every blog post has a branded image.

Guest Blogging Plan

Guest blogging is an awesome way to develop brand recognition, and earn links and references back to your site, which will drive direct traffic and help your search rankings. Guest blogging can be a time-consuming endeavour but the results are worth it. It's best to go into guest blogging with a plan.

1. Create a list of 50-100 blogs in your niche, industry, and interests of your preferred client. Do proper research; you want to be seen where your preferred clients are. Social media is a great place to find guest blogging opportunities.

Also consider participating in weekly roundups, link parties, blog challenges (participate or hold your own), or group giveaways.

These are great places to not only guest blog but make new connections, build partnerships and relationships as well as get content ideas.

2. Make it easy have content ready. Do your research on the websites and ensure you are writing in the same style and directly to their audience.

3. Create a custom email with the blog post attached, include your byline, your call to action and link to your website. You can create a loose template for emails but when sending it to personalize with blogger name and something you know about them and/or their blog.

4. Contact bloggers with your proposal. Don't be discouraged by no responses. When you get a yes, you can easily become a regular blogger with great content.

5. Decide and schedule how many proposals you want to send out on a daily / weekly basis.

For guest posting to be a successful exercise, you need to make sure that you have a quality website up, with current blog posts as well as active social media accounts.

Guest Blog Host

Stuck on creating your own content. Allow guest blogging on your blog. Build traffic, subscribers and search engine ranking with quality content.

Create a "Guest Blogging" page that lets visitors know you accept guest blog posts, the benefits and the guidelines to posting.

1. Let potential guest bloggers know the benefits of writing on your blog. Traffic to your website, the type of readers, social media exposure, etc.

2. Guidelines can include the topics you accept (be very clear), requirements such as minimum length, images, links, etc. Setting out your guidelines helps you weed out the people that are not catering to your audience.

3. Also, include a form that can be used to contact you.

Respond promptly whether it's with approval or not.

You can also solicit guest bloggers through social media connections, similar niche and industry blogs, blog directories, etc. Look for diversity, credibility, and quality content authors.

Open communication. Let guest bloggers know when their post is featured with a link to the post. This allows them to promote the post as well.

As a guest blog host, be professional and courteous. Use this as an opportunity to build relationships and create guest blogging opportunities, future partnerships and make new friends.

Blogging for SEO

All online marketing is SEO (Search Engine Optimization)

To be found online you must use the terms people are searching for to optimize your blog.

With blogging, you need to get really clear on who you are, who your preferred client is and the results you provide.

Use Search Engine Optimization (SEO) in Your Blogging Strategy

1. Do your keyword research. What terms are people using to find you, your business, your blog and your products and services? Pay attention to your Google analytics organic search terms and use Google Adwords Keyword Planner.

2. Watch industry trends and be ready to weigh in your opinion with blog posts.

3. Monitor Google trends and Twitter trends. Join the conversation with blog posts, status updates, and comments integrated with hashtags when relevant.

4. Turn long tail keywords into interesting questions / post ideas that appeal to readers. Long tail keywords are easier to rank for. It brings less traffic but has a higher conversion rate. People that use long tail keywords to search are usually ready to buy.

5. Be active. Post regularly. Use your blog to keep top of mind in your industry, in the eyes of potential clients as well as in search engines.

6. Create valuable content. If your content sucks and no one wants to engage or read it, then SEO will not help you.

While providing valuable content don't forget the importance of a keyword optimized post.

Title The most important piece of SEO real estate on any website page is the title, which tells both readers and search engines what to expect from the rest of the content. Focus on one keyword per a post and ensure you have an enticing keyword rich title. Write for readers not search engines. Go for readability while using relevant keywords in your titles.

You also have the **Meta Title** which may or may not match your post title especially when you may want to use a different title for readers than for search engines. Your title for search engines may differ in the use of keyword at the front and a simplified version to fit within the 70 characters. However, it still has to be appealing as this is what people will see on search engines.

Meta Descriptions are also important as this is what search engine users will see when your result pops up and on social media as well. The description needs to inspire users to read the blog post as well as contain the keywords used to search for it.

To edit meta data, you need to have a theme framework or plugin installed that provides a place for specific SEO meta data.

Ensure your blog utilizes meta data and incorporates open graph, schema.org and twitter cards. These tools allow social media and search engines to better classify and display information from your website.

Slug / URL Don't use automatically generated URLs. Ensure you URL is search engine friendly with keywords while being reader friendly - easy to read, and understand. If you sent only the link to someone would they be compelled to click and read? Also think compact - shorter URL's (less than 100 characters) are easier to copy, paste and share.

Links Linking is a great way to build relationships while increasing SEO rank. When you link to others not only do you get linked back you also get mentioned as well. Internal linking also helps with optimization and keeping happy readers on your website. The key to linking is optimized links with keywords - don't use "click here", say what the link is and ensure links are helpful - think resources.

Images
Rename images to describe the actual image, instead of IMG23.jpg use sunset-toronto.jpg. Take it a step further and optimize for SEO with keywords - what is the blog post about? Ensure you are uploading the proper size, instead of relying on WordPress to scale the image upload the size you want. Large images slow down the site. Finally use search engine optimized title and alt tags that use the post keywords. Pinterest uses the alt tag as the image description.

The key to using images is ensuring that it's relevant and adds value to the post.

Categories Choose 5-7 broad but relevant search engine friendly categories based on your keywords. Try to link each blog post to one category.

Tags Post tags are similar to categories but are more specific, used to describe posts in more detail and to cross reference posts. Even though tags are optional, it helps search engines categorize your posts and should be used to break down categories further. Instead of stuffing keywords in the content of your blog posts you can place all relevant keywords here.

7. Share unique content. Readers are more likely to engage with fresh content.

8. Post all your blog posts to social media. Take time to schedule your posts to other social media platforms to get backlinks and build social currency and clout. Constantly use keyword rich hashtags.

9. In addition to posting your blog posts on social media platforms use social bookmarking sites such as Delicious, StumbleUpon, Digg, and Reddit. Slowly bookmark all pages of your website not just blog posts to these sites. Just like with any other social media share others content too. Always post your blogs to your Google+ page to get instant Google cred.

10. In addition to sharing your blog posts, start guest blogging and commenting on others blogs.

11. Use blog directories.

12. Do a regular blog audit and review your top 10 most popular posts. What keywords were they optimized for? Create new content keeping these keywords in mind.

A properly search engine optimized blog can increase traffic, subscribers, leads, and sales.

Action:
List 10 keywords you can use based on keyword research.

SECTION THREE

Profit

Blogging for Sales

Monetize Your Blog

How will you make money from your blog?

If you are already running your own business, how will you incorporate blogging into your business?

A blog is not a business, it's a promotional tool. You need to monetize your blog and turn it into a business. The key to having a golden blog is having multiple streams of income.

Advertising

Display Ads - You can join an ad network such as Google AdSense, Blogads, BlogHer, Beacon Ads, Federated Media, Media.net, and Sway. These are usually Pay Per Click (PPC), you get paid when people click on the links.

Private Ads - Sell space on your website directly to advertisers to display ads. This cuts out the middle man, but you have to manage it yourself.

You call also sell space in your newsletters, podcasts, videos, and email signature.

If your objective is branding "you" and building a platform, I don't recommend advertising for two reasons. First, you are driving people away from your website. Second, you are trying to build trust and credibility. Selling other unrelated products goes against that.

Product Reviews - Provide detailed reviews of products. Can get paid for the review, can get free product to review, or can get paid by commission from the sales generated from the review.

Giveaway - Most people don't charge advertisers for hosting giveaways but you could. You would normally get a product for yourself and for the giveaway.

Sponsors - Partner with big brands for sponsored posts, sponsored social media posts, sponsored blog, or podcast and video sponsorship. Sponsored posts can also be in the form of a review.

Keep sponsored posts to a minimum, so you don't turn off readers.

Underwritten Posts or Series - Underwritten posts differ from sponsored posts in that the post topic is about whatever you want it to be (as opposed to the company's product/service), but an advertiser pays to get a "Brought to you by..." type note in the post. This also works great for podcasts and video.

Please note products you receive for free need to be reported as income on your taxes.

Don't be afraid to negotiate or offer other alternatives such as ad space in lieu of reviews or sponsorship.

Affiliate Marketing - Get commission when you sell someone else's products. Usually provide you with marketing materials such as banners and text links. Top affiliate programs include Clickbank, Shareasale, and Amazon.

Affiliate marketing is a great form of passive income as the products and marketing is already created. You don't have to worry about customer service either.

If you are using any of these methods must have full disclosure on your site that you are getting paid.

I go by this rule when promoting others:
1. Only promote things you love (and have tested or used yourself, or trust the source) and
2. Only promote things that your preferred client would be interested in

Events

Live Workshops, Seminars, Classes and Meetups - You can host your own events and have ticket sales on your website or Eventbrite. This is a great way to interact with audience, sell more services and products and build an offline following.

Conferences, Conventions, and Retreats - These events are a lot more work, but if you target the right audience, you can look at sponsorship and vendor opportunities to cover costs in addition to ticket sales.

Online Summits and Webinars - Online Summits have become very popular. Not only is it a great way to sell product and tickets but you also reach a broader audience.

You can use webinars to sell tickets too, but the most effective way is to offer free webinars and sell during the webinar.

Promoting a Business

Use your blog to drive foot traffic into your stores. Posting valuable content can increase your visibility and using creative ways to showcase your products can increase sales offline and online.

Create and Sell Your Own Products and Services

Digital Products

Ebooks - You can sell e-books directly from your own website, Amazon Kindle, E-junkie, Gum Road, or Clickbank. You can also turn your e-book into a paperback or hardback. Most authors have the most success when writing multiple books.

Courses - You can sell an online teaching course about anything with membership, subscription or a fixed amount. You can sell on your website using plugins like teachPress, Sensei, WP courseware, Study Press, CoursePress Pro, LearnPress, LearnDash. You can also sell on Udemy.

Software and Apps - Create software or apps to solve problems that your preferred client has.

Plugins and themes - Can be sold on your website or through Creative Market, Template Monster and more.

Reports, Workbooks, Guides, Blueprints, Templates, and Printables - You can sell the PDF on your website.

Images - you can sell photos and illustrations on your website or stock photo website such as Shutterstock, istockphoto

Physical Products

Books - For traditionally and self-published authors, a blog is a great platform to sell books. Whether you are selling fiction or non-fiction, you can sell directly from your blog, Amazon or other publisher. You can use Amazon CreateSpace to self-publish paperback books.

Handmade Products - Are you crafty? You can sell your creations on your own website or target a larger audience with Etsy or Handmade at Amazon. People love to buy unique items especially if you can offer customization.

Products - You can manufacture your own products to sell on your website or sell someone else's in your online shop. Consider wholesale, consignment, and drop shipping.

Merchandise- Use your brand or artwork to create t-shirts, mugs, and other merchandise to sell on your website or on-demand on Cafepress, Zazzle, etc.

Membership or Continuity Programs or Subscription

You can create recurring income by building private communities, selling premium content, adding coaching to your course or hosting a mastermind.

Services

The following can be conducted 1:1, group, online or in-person.

Coaching - Become a coach in your expertise, offer training, hand holding, encouragement, and accountability.

Consulting - Use your blog to showcase your expertise and consult with individuals and businesses.

Training - Use your expertise to offer online and offline training via your website.

Speaking - Create a speakers page to promote your speaking and book gigs.

DFY - Done For You Services

Assistant - Administrative Assistant, Personal Assistant or Virtual Assistant

Designer - Web Designer, Presentation Designer, or Marketing Collateral Designer

App Developer - Create custom apps

Social Media Manager - Manage social media accounts

Freelance Writer - Get paid to write in magazines, news, and blogs.

Selling a service is great because the startup costs are low and little to no inventory is required. However, services are not scalable if you are a one-woman shop. If you plan to go this route, be sure to plan your team. It's also why I have created books, workbooks, and e-courses to not only generate passive income but reach a broader audience while not overextending myself.

Selling services be sure to create a sales page for each service with a strong call to action. Include images of results and list clients you have worked with.

Still not sure what to sell. Look at other bloggers in your niche and see what they have had success with.

Passive Income

Pat Flynn of Smart Passive Income definition is:
"Building online businesses that take advantage of systems of automation that allow transactions, cash flow, and growth to happen without requiring a real-time presence".

The term "Passive Income" gets used a lot, especially in online marketing and people have mistaken ideas of what it actually means. Passive Income in no way means easy money or free money. Building passive income requires work up front and you still have to promote the offers whether it's your own products / services or someone else's.

Imagine having to create, market and sell a new product every month. Or being in charge of distribution and customer service by yourself. How is that effective use of your time? All this while working 1:1 with clients, and speaking gigs. When do you sleep? Eat?

Passive income for me means using your time effectively. Stop trading time for money. In conjunction with automation, you can start making money while you sleep. That is the freedom that a money making blog can give you.

Passive income offline means dividends, rental income, royalties, income from investments, and hands off income sources such as vending machines.

Online it means
- Ebook / Book
- Affiliate
- Online membership courses
- Commerce store with drop ship
- Apps
- Franchise or licensing

What passive income streams can you incorporate into your blogging business?

Your Offer

Way back in chapter one we looked at your gifts. Let's translate your gifts to your offer and what you are selling.

It's important to understand in this day and age you cannot rely on one stream of income. In my opinion, an Empowerpreneur (author, coach, or speaker) should be all three. You should be getting money from books, from coaching and from speaking. But that's not all. Turn your books, coaching programs and talks into additional income by creating the Awesome Offer.

The Awesome Offer is a mix of products and services at different price levels and a source of multiple streams of income.

Free Gifts and Content
Opt-in Offer (Awesome Free Gift)

The ideal opt-in offer should lead to selling your products and services or at minimum booking a discovery session. It can be a quality ebook, checklist, event (teleseminar or webinar) video or audio. (See Content Upgrades for more ideas)

The Discovery Session If you are offering 1:1 services, a discovery session is a great way to let potential clients get a taste of what you offer and a way for you to interview them.

Starter Series - Less than $100
Low-Priced Products, E-books or Other

This level should be introductory low priced information products that you can deliver in an automated way. These products are high-value, low risk. This is a perfect way to get people comfortable buying from you. This product should be related to your next level paying product.

Next Series - Less than $500
Your Programs (Results Oriented Systems) and Products (Do It Yourself Systems)

This level can include 4-8 week e-courses and / or 1:1 services. It can also include software or apps and other digital products to make your preferred client's life easier.

Domination Series - Less than $2,000
Higher-Priced Products, Services, and Programs

This level offers group coaching, high level e-courses, and masterminds. You can also include Done-For-You Services.

Premium Series - Over $2,000
Higher-Priced top level products, services, and programs
This level can include retreats, multi-day workshops, and VIP Days. You can also include Done-For-You Services and 1:1 or business consulting.

Continuity Programs and Memberships
You can turn or combine any of the above into this passive income stream. A few clients offer all their programs in a membership where you pay a monthly fee to be able to have unlimited access to current and future programs.

Every product should allow for upsells, and cross-sells.

EVERY OFFER MUST
- Educate
- Build Trust
- Address the Pain
- Create Urgency
- Deliver Results
- Call to Action - Ask People to Buy a Service / Product

For every offer create a great copy and graphics to promote.

Plan out your product promotions for the year. Know what products and services to promote and when. By planning out your promotions, you are able to have your marketing collateral ready and create your social media collateral, blog posts and sales pages in advance.

Sales Funnel

Many people find it hard to create a sales funnel online because a lot of online advertising only target people that want to buy now and they are trying to duplicate what others are doing. Sadly that works for companies like McDonalds, but that's only 3% of the market. At any given time 47% will never buy, and 50% will buy in the next 12 months. It's not very effective to market to all 100% when you will only get a 3% return, and it's a broken marketing system. Basically, you are attracting traffic to your website and going straight into the sales pitch. Traffic - Website - Sales.

The goal of creating clients via your website is to capture leads so you can build a relationship that will lead to not one purchase, but to multiple purchases and referrals.

Take a step back use your website to create a sales funnel that works. Traffic - Capture Leads - Nurture Leads - Convert Leads - Close, Deliver, Satisfy - Referrals.

By being clear about your preferred client you automatically eliminate the 47% who will never buy. You want your sales copy and opt-in offer to get rid of these people, you want your autoresponder to weed out these people. Don't be sad when you lose subscribers - these are the people you don't want.

Blogging is a great way to capture the attention of people that are not ready to buy today but plan to buy. Use your blog to keep people coming back and keep you top of mind for when they are ready to buy. Attract leads by using opt-in offers and content upgrades in your blog posts.

Use Va Va VooM to promote your offers when blogging. Send promotional offers to email list (and social media), make offers during live consultations, and make offers during webinars.

So now people are ready to buy from you either they are part of the 3% that come to your website or your blog reader or part of your mailing list.

Have a clear path to order. Ensure that prospective clients can find your order form / sales page quickly and easily. You never want to make them hunt for the buy button.

When visiting a lot of Empowerpreneur websites they forget to cater to the 3% that are ready to buy now, that's a quick way to lose prospects. Create a dedicated sales page where people can make a purchase now.

Don't turn away customers as they are ready to buy. Every product or service should have a Sales Hub that includes:
• Sales page
• Auto delivery
• Auto follow-up sequence

Be sure in delivery you delight and satisfy the client. You can have the best product / service but if there is a problem getting the product and they have a shitty experience it does not matter.

Definitely, include a Sales Follow Up Auto-Responder Always keep a separate list of buyers. Send a thank you / confirmation email with details for accessing the product and getting support. The following 3-5 messages reinforce the sale, help clients use the product or access the service and remind them how to get support.

BONUS: Offer an unadvertised bonus.

You can also include an upsell here as well.

Don't forget to have landing and sales page metrics where you track links, and do split testing.

The final step of your sales funnel is to have a referral and loyalty program.

Create a referral program by sending samples copies to bloggers, influencers and friends. You can also create your own affiliate program.

Traffic

Just posting valuable content is not sufficient to build a readership for your blog.

Blog traffic is important and is vital to the success of your blog.

Building blog traffic consists of a number of actions to take. You need to start with work on what I call your back-end:
- Branding (visually appealing, images, and your voice)
- Good Web Design (functionality, easy navigation)
- Good Content (speaks directly to your avatar, viral content, evergreen content)

Not only you are search engine optimizing each post, but you also want to optimize your website. Spend a little extra time keyword researching blog posts. Use categories and tags to identify and classify blog content.

Another great SEO tactic is to reference your own posts and those of others, especially influencers.

Search engines love new content, so consistency and frequency in posting are very important. Creating and sticking to a schedule is vital.

Be a good guest, guest blogging and commenting on others blogs can help kickstart traffic to your blog.

Set up a RSS feed and encourage subscriptions. Subscribers will get a notification every time you publish a post.

Each blog post needs to be promoted.
- Social Media
- Discussion Forums
- Email Marketing
- Email Signature
- Blog Parties

Repurpose content linking back to the original

Presentation - Slideshare
Video - YouTube and Vimeo

Use analytics to review traffic sources and searched terms. You can generate more traffic by sharing and re-sharing blog posts from where you get the most traffic. Create blog posts based on search users use to find you is a great way to increase your visitors and how long they stay on your website.

Lastly include your blog / website on all your offline marketing materials such as brochures, business cards, flyers, etc. All communication should list your blog URL.

Good Web Design

There is no doubt that convincing your prospects to make a purchase from your website is a hard job! But have you ever considered that you could be making the process more difficult? This is especially true if your site is poorly designed and your prospective clients don't have a clear and easy path to the order button!

Landing Pages
Landing pages are dedicated opt-in or sales pages that have no menu, header, logo or other distractions. Utilize landing pages to place emphasis on what you are promoting. Ensure your landing page has only one clear call to action.

Resource Page
Provide a free resources page. This is a great opportunity to not only promote your own products and services but also tools that your preferred clients can use too. A resource page is

also a money maker for any affiliate products that you are promoting.

Every product should have one or more free opt-ins that promote the product, and the resource page is a great way to showcase these opt-ins.

Sidebar

Don't forget to utilize the sidebar. With some awesome images of your products and affiliate products, you can start selling. Use your sidebar and footer to draw attention to your opt-ins and products. Also, spotlight your most popular posts. People forget that these areas can also be used for navigation.

People forget to promote their website / blog. Let people know they can find valuable information via your website by reading your blog. When talking to people promote it and use your marketing collateral to promote it.

Print Materials
- Business Card
- Flyers
- Postcards
- Trade Show Banners
- Thank you cards
- Appointment cards
- Brochures
- Presentation Folders
- Letterhead
- Envelopes
- Invoices

Call to Action

Most bloggers fail to make it a business because they think providing valuable content is enough. Posting regular Awesome content is great, but it's not going to bring you the big bucks. Valuable content can drive visitors, and even engagement but alone won't drive sales. You need to **encourage readers to take action.**

1. Engage
2. Subscribe
3. Buy

Use a targeted call-to-action related to your business goals.

Based on your monthly goals develop a call to action for each blog post. **Determine what you want readers to do after reading your blog posts.** Then incorporate a contextually relevant call-to-action in each article.

What do you want people to do? Tell them!

Not using a call to action on your blog is a missed opportunity and defeats the purpose of blogging for business.

What do you want your followers to do? Call, Email, Download or Purchase? Tell followers what you want them to do. With each post add a call to action. Click here, like, comment, share, etc.

It can be subtle such as adding links to your products in your posts.

Use **VaVaVoom** to create a mix of promotional posts, value add posts (printables and downloads) and information.

Communicate urgency in your promotional posts - Most
people react out of fear of missing out

- Now
- Today
- Act now
- Limited time only
- Limited quantity
- Enter soon
- On sale
- This week only
- Don' miss out
- Etc.

Awesome Gift

The quickest way to monetize your blog is to create your list.
And the quickest way to build your list is with an Awesome
Gift. The Opt-in aka the Awesome Gift: Ebook, Checklist,
Event (Teleseminar, Webinar or Live Event, Video or Audio
Class) is a great way to capture leads and build your list.

The Free Offer - Opt-in - Awesome Gift is an INCENTIVE.
The offer must be valuable and relevant to your preferred
client.
Don't offer crap, a real value of at least $100 goes a long way of
turning the subscriber into a buyer.
You need to build a list to build relationships and nurture
loyalty

REMEMBER Like, Know and Trust which leads to sales
Drive more traffic to the list building hub

Create more free content and hubs as needed
Track and test for your most successful offers and traffic sources

Create a List Building Hub

Opt-in Boxes - Have an Opt-in form above the fold and/or in the top right corner, use an action popup (on entry and/or exit)

Opt-in Page - Use a focused landing page to convert readers. A landing page removes other distractions that hinder reader action and has only one call to action. This dedicated landing page can be used for traffic from advertising and social media.

Confirmation Page / Thank-you Page - Thank and welcome them, inform them that the registration is complete and deliver free content.

Autoresponder Emails - Nurture Leads and Build Relationships

Create a 7-12 message autoresponder for your List Building Hub. Ensure that emails are created to build trust and provide valuable information. Use your autoresponder sequence to educate.

Next, use this opportunity to promote your offers, affiliate programs, launch products and services, offer other freebies, invite feedback, and drive traffic to your blog. Remember **VaVaVoom**.

PROMOTE YOUR FREE OFFER

1 - Email signature in your emails

2 - Newsletter

3 - Other people's newsletters

4 - Your website

5 - Articles

6 - Social Media and Social Media Ads

7 - Business Card

8 – Teleseminars

9 – Video

10 – Blog Posts Create specific blog posts that specifically ask readers to subscribe to your mailing list or get their Awesome Gift. Also, create posts with opt-in content upgrades.

Don't Make These List Building Mistakes

- Adding people without permission
- Using Outlook or Gmail to manage your list.
- Hiding who you are or what you're sending behind a tricky subject line or a fake name.
- No contact information in every email (Address and phone number)
- No opt-out option
- Not honouring opt-out
- No tracking. Track and test open rates on types of subjects/content, click-through rates on calls-to-action and sales
- No consistency
- Bad subject lines that don't entice readers to open your emails
- No calls to action such as clicking the links in your email or attending your events or buy your products and services
- No engagement, not encouraging readers to interact and reply

- Too much promotion. Provide a mix of content and promotion - remember VaVaVooM

Sales Pages

The leap from having a wonderful blog - a showcase of just articles to actually having sales is incorporating dedicated sales pages. Pages that are linked to from blog posts and that also can be used as standalone landing pages.

Your offer should have a compelling headline, clear and enticing images and an easy way to purchase.

Every Offer Must Haves
- Benefits - Results / What's in It For Me
- Bonuses
- Testimonials
- Call to Action
- Multiple Payment Options
- Guarantees - The majority of customers will not request a refund, especially if you are offering a quality product. However, if they do request a refund make sure the process is quick and easy as well.

Ensure Your Sales Page Answers The Most Important Questions
- What is this product/service?
- Why do I need it?
- When do I get results?
- How do I order the product/service?
- When does the product/service arrive?
- How much is it?
- What is included?
- Is there a guarantee or return policy?

- Why is this different from Joe Schmoe's product/service?
- Does it come in different colors?

Include Frequently Asked Questions on Your Sales Page

When a prospect is interested in what you offer as a product/service, she comes to the table with questions. Online you're not there to answer those questions so you have to anticipate what those questions might be to overcome potential objections in the copy. Those are the frequently asked questions or FAQs section.

- Who?
- What?
- Why?
- When?
- Where?
- How?
- How much?
- Offer?
- Guarantee?
- Objections?

Social Proof

Providing social proof is very important to selling online as it adds another layer of credibility for people to trust you. Remember your website / blog may be your first impression.

If you have prominent public relations, where you are featured include that on your website.

If you have guest blogged for others or have featured articles, let people know where to find you.

Showcase your "as seen" section on your home page and your about page.

And last but not least ensure you get permission from your list of happy clients to include their testimonials on your website in a prominent place. Include testimonials on your home page, about page, sidebar and of course on your sales pages. 2-3 short testimonials from clients who think you and your services are AWESOME! Testimonials should speak to your expertise and ability to get results. Always ask tor a testimonial.

Promotions & Self Promotion

Some people will get so caught up in providing valuable information that they forget to sell.

Use your blog content to promote and presell – not only to provide content.

Increase your blog's effectiveness at closing sales by providing useful product information such as how-to's, instructions and other product support.

Allow your blog to be a 24/7 customer service hub. Create a category that can be linked to in your menu or sidebar that provides useful information on working with you, and using your products and services.

Consider a "Frequently Asked Questions" - FAQ section that you can add to and update.
Use your blog to create product announcements, run launch campaigns, refer and mention your products and services, and

directly ask for the sale. Review your marketing calendar and create posts to support your campaigns.

Use your blog to run a feasibility test before you create products and services. Create product images, and sales page before you invest in product creation to see if interest is there. Use the images, sales pages, and ads to drum up interest and presell.

Your blog can be the most effective tool for your self-promotion. Your blog can:
- Establish credibly
- Show your expertise
- Show what it's like to work with you
- Show your personality
- Share your work
- Tell your story

Blogging for Engagement

Make Your Blog Shareable

Blogging is not just a broadcast channel. You want to be able to get readers to interact and share your blog posts.

There are three aspects to blog engagement
1. Make your blog shareable
2. Be active
3. Effective use of social media.

As part of your social media strategy your blog editorial content calendar includes which social media platforms you plan to share the post on, when you will share and how often.

I recommend sharing on the date you publish, a week later and a month later. It's good to also create a plan on how you will share old blog posts.

Search engines love blogs; unique and frequent content is a great way to get ranked in search engines. Plan each post to promote your opt-ins and products and services. Mix in regular blog posts with evergreen blog posts (long, unique, and informative), controversial blog posts (make a stand and say what's on your mind) and trendy blog posts.

Make Your Blog Shareable

- Awesome content
- Easy to read posts (formatted with headings bullets, bold, etc.)
- Free resources, downloads, and printables
- Search Engine Optimize (SEO) all posts
- Branded image with each post
- Call to action with each post
- Share buttons on all posts
- Embed Facebook updates in posts
- Embed Pinterest boards or images updates in posts
- Embed Instagram images in posts
- Use click to tweet in posts
- Pinit Button
- Social Media profile links
- Contact page
- Search Box
- RSS Feed Subscription
- Respond to blog posts comments in a timely manner
- Opt-in in multiple places

Monitor and track your blog using analytic tools such as Google Analytics. Measure how much traffic you get from each social media platform to your blog. Go a step further and track conversions.

Action: Optimize your blog for social media.

Be Active

Your blog is not set it and forget it. It's nice to schedule posts and promote your products but you also want to create engagement by being active.

Being blog active means engaging on your own blog via comments, others blogs, and social media.

Real Interaction
Allow comments on your website - Ask for and reward engagement.
Be sure to respond to any comments on your blog. Encourage comments by asking your readers for their opinions. Take time to not only respond but let them know you appreciate it with a quick thank-you. Also if someone is commenting visit their sites, leave a comment back and share their blog posts on social media.

Blog Commenting
To get your blog seen and heard and to increase engagement commit to guest posting and commenting on others blogs.

Provide valuable content via comments on other blogs related to your niche. Think branding when creating your username and links.

Create a commenting plan.
1. Find and comment on blogs that cater to your niche.
2. How many comments do you plan to leave per day?
3. Ensure comments are thoughtful and relevant.

Make Connections

Blog comment and share with prospects, influencers, supplier, and friends. Not everyone will connect with you on your blog or your email list. Use your blog to open conversation, send a link with a message "I thought this would be of interest to you". Your blog can be an effective networking tool.

Link to others blog posts as reference points and for further information in your blog posts. BE AN EXPERT!

Take Advantage of Blog Syndication

Content syndication is the process of pushing your blog content out into third-party sites, either as a full article, snippet, link, or thumbnail. Beware of Duplicate Content - SEO Impact. Search Engines don't like duplicate content and penalize you or will give credit to the most popular website. If it's not an original post add "Original post found on your URL (of the original post)" or something similar. Blog syndication can drive more traffic and engagement and boost your reputation and visibility.

Don't Make this Mistake

I'm sure you have been to blogs where the owner does not respond to comments. You want to make sure that you monitor comments and be especially attentive to comments regarding your products, services and purchases.

Social Media Engagement 15 Minutes a Day

To Promote Your Blog Find Out Where Your Preferred Readers Hang Out on Social Media

1. Share the blog post URL on every social media platform. Create unique "teasers" for each platform (Facebook, Twitter, LinkedIn, Google+, Pinterest, and Instagram). Using tools such as Buffer and Hootsuite you can schedule your blog posts on social media.

2. Share the blog post image.
For each blog post create shareable social media images. Each social media platform has its own dimensions. (**Download the social media cheat sheet included in the Workbook**)

For regular blog posts create at least 3 images. One image that fits in with your branded blog. Two images for your dominate social media platform. For example, if you get the most traffic from Pinterest create the images for Pinterest. Use different calls to actions, different images, etc.

For promotions such as product launches, giveaways, etc., I recommend that each social media platform has its own image.

3. Utilize the sharing tools on your blog such as click to tweet and the pin button.

4. Create Conversation
When you post especially on Facebook ask a question to encourage engagement such as feedback, like and shares.

5. Custom hashtags

Use popular hashtags to get your posts found. Also, create custom hashtags to promote your brand and your blog post.

6. Don't be a spammer.

Don't simply drive-by spamming leaving your links. Spend time interacting and making friends. Add value - consistent quality content and engagement will increase fans and traffic.

7. Join the conversation on social media.

Participate in groups, communities and chats. On a weekly basis be seen and heard by participating. Showcase your expertise by answering questions.

8. Interact

Don't just post and leave. Interact with every single comment. Respond promptly. Immerse yourself in the conversation primarily if you started it with your blog post.

9. Become a Curator

Not only do you share your own content, share others. Use your social media to be a source of information on your topic, in your industry, etc.

10. Don't forget Social Bookmarking

Post your blog posts on social bookmarking website like Delicious, StumbleUpon, Digg and Reddit.

11. Don't Forget Forums

Find at least one forum where your preferred client is, build engagement and answer questions. Add value with useful information. Promote your blog with link in your signature.

12. Create a Social Media Marketing Plan that includes posting quotes, questions, tips, photos, behind-the-scene, testimonials, your products and services, etc. Use your editorial calendar to schedule social media and use batching on a weekly, bi-weekly, or monthly basis.

Engagement in 15 Minutes A Day

On a daily basis check your feed to find posts that are either beneficial to your Awesome Nation or stand out on a personal level.

1. Share / Retweet / Pin

2. Like posts of people in your network, influencers, and clients

3. Comment / Reply

4. Respond to any communication via private message, or commenting on your posts.
5. Review posts in communities and groups to share, like, and comment on

6. Status updates if applicable

If you have a campaign or promotion running, 15 minutes of engagement can turn into an hour of engagement or more.

Use social media as an inspiration for posts on your blog. By observing what performs well and earns engagement, you can tailor your content.

Blog Metrics

How do you know blogging is working? Besides seeing actual sales - money in hand, you can track and monitor your blogging and overall online marketing success.

Master analytics, learn to read and understand reports. Analytics is invaluable to your blogs growth and success. Blog metrics is your guide to understanding what's working and what's not working, how you can improve and give readers what they want.

Know your blog stats to keep creating awesome content!
- How many readers per day on average visit your blog?
- What are your top three most viewed blog posts?
- What are your posts with the most comments?
- How many leads do you generate?

Know Your Top 5
- Top 5 popular blog posts
- Top 5 most commented blog posts
- Top 5 blog posts with the most social media engagement

On a weekly, monthly, quarterly and annual basis review your online metrics.

Learn more about your return on investment (ROI – time and money) as well as which blog posts brings the most traffic, engagement, and conversion.

Always track the results of your blog posts. Once you know what type of content your audience interacts with, you can plan the type of information you are sharing as well as carefully create specific calls to action to increase leads and sales.

1. Traffic
Knowing which blog posts receive the highest number of views can help you determine the type of content to post.

Visitors Track visitors, unique visitors, where they come from and what sections they go to.

Content Marketing Pageviews show the number of times your blog has been viewed over a specific period of time. This number includes new visitors and returning readers alike. You can track per day & per month (& versus prior period) of specific pages. Also review downloads, clicks on links, RSS signups, email signups, and where readers exit.

Referral Tracking. Know who sends traffic your way. This enables you to see which websites most refer readers to your blog. Learn if your SEO efforts are working, and what social media sites send the most traffic. Out of all the stats this one lets you know if your online marketing is working and what methods are worth investing your time in.

2. Conversion
See what blog posts results in getting leads. Use a call-to-action, content upgrades and other opt-ins to get people motivated and build your list.

3. Sales
See what blog posts results in getting actual sales. Use a call-to-action, custom promotion codes and targeted landing pages

to help lead readers to take appropriate action and for tracking beyond metrics.

4. Engagement

In conjunction with popular posts by traffic, you also want to review popular posts by engagement.

Time Spent on Site. See how much time people are spending on your blog when they visit. If your bounce rate is high and people are not spending time on your blog it's time to review why.

Bounce Rate. A low bounce rate means that people are spending time on your site and reading several posts when they visit.

Review blog comments, shares, likes and comments on social media.

How many people are visiting your blog from social media and are they engaging on your website? Learn which blog posts do well on social media. Use Google Analytics in conjunction with Bitly, Buffer, Hootsuite or other reporting tools and the social media platform analytics to track and monitor your social media success.

5. SEO

Find out which keyword searches lead readers to your blog. Create blogs posts around popular keyword searches to your website. Also use your blog to answer search questions.

Make an effort to SEO your blog with relevant keywords and inbound links to improve your keyword ranking.

Review your weekly, monthly and yearly stats to learn how to improve your blogging strategy. Most analytics programs allow you to specify a certain period of time to display a graph charting the growth of your blog. This way, you can review the past three months, the past year, or the growth of your blog since its beginning.

Tracking is crucial, especially when using content marketing. You want to keep track of where people are coming from and what messages are resonating and making people take action.

Don't forget to evaluate.
Every month and quarter see if you have achieved the goals you set out for yourself. Set new goals and benchmarks. Test and adjust strategy as needed

Blog Maintenance

Blogging Maintenance is a very important to running a successful and healthy blog.

Unless your tech savvy, it's useful to at least have someone to help you with any blog backend issues. While creating content is at the heart of blogging, technical support is necessary to improve your blog's performance and ensure everything works right.

Make sure your blog is configured correctly to ensure it has a strong foundation. Ideally, your blog should be integrated with your website.

It's important to review your blog maintenance on a monthly basis (**Blog Maintenance Worksheet included in Workbook**)

Keep your software up-to-date and secure. This means using the latest version of your software (i.e., WordPress) and taking other security measures. For example, not using "admin" for your administrator's username. One of the many reasons to use WordPress is because it has free regular software updates for security and feature enhancements.

Even though WordPress is awesome you need additional tools for optimal functionality such as analytics, social media sharing and others to run your website. Configure your blog for plugins. This also includes choosing the best plugins for these services.

Keep your plugins updated Just like your WordPress, you need to keep the plugins you've installed up to date as well. By keeping compatible with the latest WordPress update you avoid security breeches and a broken website.

Reduce plugins. While plug-ins are great for solving problems, they take time to load, hinder performance and could add security vulnerabilities. Only have installed plugins that are essential to running your website, remove any unused plugins.

Maximize your blog speed. Slow websites have many repercussions such as how long visitors stay on your website (Remember 3 seconds) and low search rankings.

On a regular basis clean out and optimize your blog's database.

BAD LINKS SUCK! No one wants to have broken links on their website. The more links you have both external and internal the more you should be checking.
Broken links happen.
External website page is removed or renamed
Misspelling in the link
Mistake when posting link
Sometimes a visitor will come to your site based on a link that does not exist. That is when you use error messages to your benefit and brand your 404 and 403 pages.
When you have too many broken links, visitors get frustrated and won't return. It looks like you don't care about your site - NEGLECT and you lose SEO status when search engines can't find a page and stops search engines from completely indexing your site - DEVALUES SEO.

Maintain your blog comments regularly. Clear out any spam that's been caught by your spam filter and don't miss replying to any visitors that have replied to your blog posts.

Remember to Backup!

This is without a doubt something that's neglected by most website owners. They don't realize that if something happened and their website goes down (as rare that it happens) that they have nothing backed up.

The best way to backup is to use a backup plugin such as Vaultpress or Backup Buddy. Plugins like these can be installed and setup so backups are created automatically and saved to your hosting server or hard drive for a fee.

In addition to being a good practice in case you have a technical problem, having a full backup allows you to move your site at any time.

CONCLUSION

Blogging Mistakes

Blogging is not the easiest way to promote your business and make money. It's easy to get discouraged. BUT don't give up. This book is meant to help you if you are making these blogging mistakes.

1. You Hate Writing
- Outsource
- Podcast
- Vlogging (Video)
- Curate - Posts that refer to other blogs
- Get Guest Bloggers

2. Writers Block
- Review your blog schedule. Are you trying to write too much?
- Try the 52 Week brainstorm
- Research. Check out how what's popping on Social Media to see what others are blogging about.
- Poll your audience.
- Mind Map and Brainstorming Sessions - What problems do your clients have - related and unrelated? What solutions can you provide or recommend?
- Reread section on writers block to get more ideas.

3. No Audience
- Promote you blog on Social Media
- Build a community of friends or social media buddies to support each other:
    - Visit blogs of each others blogs
    - Comment on each others blogs
- Join a blog challenge

4. No Engagement
- Use call to action
- Encourage commenting and sharing (See Blog Engagement Section)
- Commenting Circles - join groups on social media that allows people to share their blogs and encourage commenting on each others blog
- Listen to your readers and clients and give them what they want. Review blog comments, emails, and analytic reports to see what is working and what's not. Use feedback both good and bad to make you blog better.

Conclusion

Build your blog around your passion, create a plan and start seeing profits.

It's rare for a blog to be an overnight success. It's hard to get traffic and comments especially when you first start out. Don't Give Up!

Your blog is a part of your marketing and can become a great source of income. Your blog is a work in process and can only get better the more you blog.
By reading this book you have created an awesome blog plan but nothing is set in stone. Adapt as you go. Learn to be flexible and get your cues from readers and analytics on how to grow your blog.
Your blog is not done. It will never be finished. It is a growing part of your business that you can experiment with, develop and even change as your business grows.

Good Luck with Your Blog!

THANK-YOU

HOPE YOU ENJOYED READING
FALL IN LOVE WITH BLOGGING
FROM PASSION TO PLAN TO PROFIT

PLEASE LEAVE A REVIEW ON AMAZON

The exercises in this book can be found in the **Fall in Love with Blogging Workbook**.

DOWNLOAD YOUR COPY OF THE 76 PAGE FALL IN LOVE WITH BLOGGING WORKBOOK
http://bit.ly/love-blogging-workbook

GET YOUR FREE BLOGGING BONUSES!
http://bit.ly/love-blogging-bonus

ALSO LOOK OUT FOR
Authentic Marketing – The Three E's of Online Marketing: Ethical, Effortless, Engaging

Connect with Dwainia Grey on LinkedIn, Google+, Facebook, Twitter, Pinterest and Instagram
dwainiagrey.me

BONUS

Join the **Empowerpreneur League** Facebook Group to network with others for support, feedback, brainstorming, growth and tips. This group is 100% Free and made up of Empowerpreneurs across the world.
http://bit.ly/empowerpreneur-league

You can also join us on LinkedIn.
http://bit.ly/empowerpreneur-marketing

BE SURE TO GRAB YOUR COPIES
- Social Media Marketing: How to Master Engagement in 15 Minutes a Day -
- Social Media Marketing:
How to Master Engagement in 15 Minutes a Day
Workbook and Planner-
- Facebook Media Marketing
Workbook and Planner-
- Google+ Workbook and Planner -
- LinkedIn Workbook and Planner -
- Twitter Workbook and Planner -
- Pinterest Workbook and Planner -
- Instagram Workbook and Planner

www.ingramcontent.com/pod-product-compliance
Lightning Source LLC
Chambersburg PA
CBHW060615200326
41521CB00007B/780